Everyday Cooking

Sandra Katanic

Thank you for
your support,
happy cooking!
love
Sandra

Everyday Cooking with Sandra Katanic

http://www.sandrakatanic.com/

ISBN: 978-0-9917433-1-5

Book design by Sarah E. Holroyd (http://sleepingcatbooks.com)
Cover photograph by Annalena Photography
Interior photography by Amanda Gobatto, Digital Girl Consulting (www.DigitalGirlConsulting.com)

Dedication

This book has been a life long dream of mine. I have had a lot of people who have inspired me over many years including my mom Emilia and my grandmother Marija Heller. I want to thank my sister Liz for being my first audience when I was 10. I used to make her watch me cook, comment and clap at the end of my shows.

This book has been a big production for many years and I could not have done it without my wonderful team. Thank you to my friend and amazing photographer Amanda Gobatto for your beautiful eye for detail and making every angle of each dish looks its best. Thank you for always making me follow my gut, your wisdom and friendship. None of this would have been possible without you.

Thank you Colleen Lindberg for your guidance, advice and keeping me on track. Your expertise has made this journey come to fruition, I am forever grateful.

Last my family and my hero, my husband Moma Katanic. I have become the person I am today because of you. You have always supported me in everything I do, all my ideas, wishes and dreams. To my 3 boys who have been my taste testers and biggest critics, thank you for tolerating me on my crazy busy days when I was not always the easiest person to deal with. Life has been fun and happy cooking for all of you. Thank you from the bottom of my heart.

Table of Contents

Foreword

In the spirit of Sandra Katanic's latest "Everyday Cooking," a clear and complete vision is painted for what modern, family-style home cooking should look like: comforting, inclusive, practical, and often vegetable-focused with a local and seasonal approach. Chef Sandra's first cookbook offers a small peak at the ways she cooks and entertains at home. With a focus on using exquisite ingredients, regional when possible, Sandra believes in cooking generously. Her passion lies in how food brings friends and families together, food that is easy to share. Celebrating that very ethos, Sandra explores the unfussy, nourishing food that would be a delight to have waiting for you when you get home. This cookbook is unapologetic in its simplicity, yet exudes brilliant and wholesome flavours that you'll make for every picnic, party, and soirée for years to come.

Sandra Berardi
Co-Owner of Michael-Angelo's

Introduction

This has been a dream of mine since childhood. As a young child, I would present dinners with my family, like I was on a cooking show. My audience would consist of my sister, who at the end was required to clap. I was always drawn to cooking and food and did everything I could to be creative in this space as a young child.

My passion for food came at an early age, however my mother would never let me cook in the kitchen because she didn't want me to make a mess. So, I got creative with my easy bake oven and the radiator in my room. I would take items from the fridge, chop them up and then use them to make soups. My friends would come over and I would share my passion for cooking with them. As I grew into my teenage years I would try to watch as many cooking shows as possible and, as you know, at the time there weren't cooking channels like there are today. However, every Saturday morning, I would watch PBS for the cooking shows while others were watching cartoons. In other instances, when we would go to the library, I could be found sifting through cook books, dreaming about the days I eventually would start to cook.

At the age of 17, I started to refine my skills and actually began to cook. This time using a stove! Everything that I have done is self taught and all of my recipes are refined personally. I didn't go to culinary arts school, nor did I work in a restaurant kitchen. Everything that I have created has come from my personal home. Some people have asked me why I didn't pursue formal education in this field, and the truth is, at the time, money was tight. I married the love of my life at a young age, we started having a family and then life happened. I loved cooking for people but I never wanted to own a restaurant or pursue a traditional chef position, as my love for food was in the teaching and helping people to cook for themselves. It wasn't just about feeding people to feed people. Back in the day we didn't have social media, there was no YouTube and you couldn't find recipes online. It's amazing how the times have changed and what we have access to for information on cooking and recipes nowadays.

In 2013, I left my corporate job and started up a Facebook page in the hopes to be able to help people that were in my position. I was hoping to connect with very busy people with kids, maybe they commute and they might be overwhelmed with getting everything done. My tips and recipes would make things easier for them.

My passion is cooking with whole foods and easy, simple recipes that are delicious. Through this online channel, I have also taught people how to grocery shop properly: how to find items on sale, prepare for the week so you can use ingredients that go together or buy in bulk to save on time and money. Throughout this process, my love for information came through, I become hooked on personal development from books, events and audio programs. I simply could not get enough. I established a business driven mindset and began hoping and dreaming about this whole business coming to life.

In the beginning, I did some catering as well as making meals for people. Over time, my passion wasn't in the catering side of the business. I did love helping people eat healthier with their everyday meals, but my passion was in teaching people how to do it themselves. Through that, the decision to go strictly online came about. I was in a position where I could focus on creating an online presence and putting out recipes and tips on a weekly basis. I enjoy talking about how to cook with a variety food items or kitchen essentials that should be in every home and bringing it back to the basics by helping people eat healthier with their everyday meals.

More than 20 years ago, I dreamed about making my own cook book. While I sat in the libraries reading over the recipes, I said to myself "one day you will have your own". Earlier in 2017, this dream started to come alive. This dream was a burning desire for me, however I didn't have the logistics in place to do it on my own. I knew the recipes I would put in it and the way I wanted it to look, but I didn't know how to put it together. I believe that everything happens for a reason. When I made the decision to do this, a team came behind me to help. With focus and a lot of dedication, what you see today was a work of art and a combination of many great talents. Now I have a cook book which you are reading that is the start of many more to come.

I cook from the heart, I cook using my own palette and I often use a trial and error method. I love to travel and incorporate other foods from different cultures. I love fusion cooking. A lot of how I cook is continental European with French flares and Eastern European styles. Blending different cultures using food is something that I really love.

This book is all about cooking with everyday ingredients, using simple recipes to make cooking easy. It features how I like to cook during the week as well as tips and tricks to save time, make substitutions and pre-plan. Most of the recipes are classic dishes with my own spin. Please enjoy this book and enjoy cooking.

From the love of my kitchen to yours,

Sandra

Tips and Tricks

My philosophy in the kitchen is to make cooking simple and easy. I also believe that recipes can be tweaked according to taste and using substitutions when needed. Here are some of my tips that I use and follow regularly.

What is Passata? Passata is strained tomatoes that usually come in a 1 litre jar. There are no added flavours such as garlic or basil. If you cannot find Passata, you can substitute with canned crushed tomatoes or any strained tomato.

What is Vegeta? Vegeta is a type of bouillon powder used throughout Europe. It is found in almost all grocery stores in the soup section. It is made of a salt base with dried onion, carrot and celery. Its flavour is similar to a vegetable broth. I use Vegeta in almost everything. If you cannot find Vegeta you can substitute with a bouillon cube.

What is deglazing? Deglazing is basically using a liquid to release brown bits from a pan when browning meat, sautéing or caramelizing onions. Wine, broth and water can be used in small amounts to lift the brown bits. The process helps to add flavour back into the food.

Buy meat in bulk. I always buy meat that is on sale. Sometimes, I like to create two dishes using one package of meat. For example, if I buy a whole pork loin, I like to split it into three parts. I will use one part for a roast, second part to cut into cutlets and grill on the BBQ and the third part I cut into cubes for a stew. When I buy ground beef, I always buy approximately two pounds. From this, I can make Stuffed Peppers, Bolognese Sauce and Beef and Potato Moussaka. I also like to roast two chickens at a time. One chicken we will each for dinner, the second chicken I use to add to salads and sandwiches.

What is Tempering? This is the process of combining two ingredients of different temperatures. The two ingredients are combined slowly so that they both combine without separating. Tempering sour cream for the leek and potato soup is done by adding a ladle of soup to the sour cream and stirring the two together to make the sour cream warm gradually and stay a consistent texture. If you were to add sour cream directly to the pot of soup without tempering, the sour cream could split and you would have visible white bits, rather than a smooth blended soup. Tempering is also used for eggs and chocolate.

What do I do with leftovers? I love leftovers! Usually when I have leftovers, like 2-3 pieces of meat, it is not enough to feed my family of 5 but it is enough to add to something as part of a new dish. For example if I have one leftover steak or chicken breast, I like to it in any of the following:

- pasta sauce
- soup
- stew
- fritatta
- stir fry
- sandwiches
- salads

Tip: I always double up on pulled pork, meatloaf, soups, pasta dishes and stews. These all freeze very well and always taste and look delicious when warmed up.

How to store herbs? We have all bought a bunch of fresh herbs, but have not needed the full bunch. Do not discard those herbs, dry and freeze for future use. The best herbs used dried are rosemary, thyme, oregano and bay leaves. I wash and pat dry those herbs and lay them out on a dishcloth in a dry area for about a week. They will completely dry out during this time. I then remove the leaves from the stems and store in a glass jar. The best herbs to freeze are parsley, dill, and coriander. Once frozen, they retain their fresh flavour and when added into food, they taste just like they were out of the fridge. I feel that dried parsley, dill and coriander do not taste the same when dried. To freeze, wash and dry the herbs, remove from stems and chop. Store in freezer bags. Add to food from frozen.

SUBSTITUTIONS:

Ground Beef: For any recipes that call for ground beef, you can always substitute any meat such as ground chicken, turkey, pork or lamb. The flavour is different, but it is the same texture.

Onions: If a salad calls for Vidalia onions and you are out, you can always use red onion, scallions, Spanish onion or shallots.

Salad Greens: You can use any type of lettuce you like. If you do not like or can't find arugula, no problem, just use your favourite variety instead. Salads are so versatile and often people have a personal preference. If there is an ingredient you love, add it, and if there is something you don't like, just take it out of the recipe.

Dairy: If a recipe calls for milk you can use plain, unsweetened nut milks or broth. For a creamy pasta sauce you can always use sour cream or cream cheese, if you do not have time to make a béchamel sauce. This is a fast, easy cut to making a delicious cream sauce.

ALL RECIPES IN THIS BOOK ARE FAMILY SIZE, FEEDING 4-5 PEOPLE

Kitchen Essentials

In every kitchen there is a need for basic ingredients that should always be stocked.

Here are two lists of pantry and fridge essentials that I always have in my kitchen.

Pantry

Flour
Corn Starch
Pasta
Long grain rice, white and basmati
Arborio rice
Quinoa
Extra Virgin Olive Oil
Coconut Oil
Sunflower Oil
Balsamic Vinegar
White Balsamic Vinegar
Apple Cider Vinegar
Soy Sauce
Honey
Onions
Garlic
Ginger
Yellow Flesh Potatoes
Beans
Chick Peas
Lentils
Crushed Tomatoes
Tomato Paste

Spices

Salt
Pepper
Rosemary
Thyme
Oregano
Bay Leaves
Vegeta
Paprika
Smoked Paprika
Chili Flakes
Cumin

Fridge

Carrots
Celery
Parsley
Sour Cream and Yogurt
Dijon Mustard
Mayonnaise
Sriracha Sauce
Eggs
Butter
Jam
Feta and Cheddar Cheese

Soups and Stews

Minestrone Soup
Leak and Potato Soup
Miso Soup
Harvest Stew
Bean Stew with Smoked Pork
Fresh Green Pea Soup
Chicken and Pea Stew
Beef Goulash
Tomato and Pesto Soup
Butternut Squash Soup

Minestrone Soup

2 carrots, thinly sliced
2 onions, diced
2 celery stalks, diced
1 can white beans
½ pound green beans, trimmed and cut in half
1 can diced tomatoes
2 cups fresh spinach
2-3 Tbsp Vegeta
3 bay leaves
1 tsp pepper
1 tsp oregano
1 tsp dried thyme
¼ cup oil
4-6 cups of water
parmesan (optional)

In a stock pot, sauté carrots, onions and celery in oil for 10 minutes. Add white beans and green beans, tomatoes and seasonings. Cover with 4-6 cups of water (enough to cover the vegetables) and simmer for 30 minutes. At the end, add spinach and remove from heat. Serve with a tsp of grated parmesan (optional).

Leek and Potato Soup

1 bunch of leeks, sliced
3 stalks celery, chopped
1 onion, diced
8 potatoes, peeled and cubed
3 bay leaves
3 Tbsp oil
12 cups water
1 cup sour cream
1 cup fresh parsley, chopped
1 Tbsp Vegeta

Sauté leeks and onions for 5 minutes. Add celery, bay leaves, potatoes, water and Vegeta. Simmer on low for 35 minutes. When done, remove bay leaves and use an immersion blender to purée until very smooth. Add sour cream to bowl and add 1 cup of soup to temper the sour cream. Mix well, then combine sour cream mixture to soup and blend again. Add parsley and serve.

Miso Soup

4 Tbsp white miso paste
4 cups chicken stock
4 cups water
1 green onion, sliced thinly
1 cup firm tofu, cubed in ½ inch pieces
½ cup sliced button mushrooms or enoki mushrooms

Add miso to stockpot and add stock and water and bring to a boil. Reduce to low and stir so all miso paste is dissolved. Add onion, mushrooms and tofu and serve.

Harvest Stew

3 large onions, diced
4 carrots, peeled and thinly sliced
1 red bell pepper, diced
3 celery stalks, diced
1 pound mushrooms, sliced
8 potatoes, peeled and cut into 1 inch cubes
2 pounds of meat of choice (stewing beef, chicken or pork loin)
salt, pepper and Vegeta to taste
6 sprigs, fresh thyme
4 bay leaves
1 pound diced fresh tomatoes or 1 large can diced tomatoes
3 Tbsp oil
Water to cover

In oil, brown meat on all sides and set aside. In oil, sauté onions for 5 minutes. Add carrots, celery, peppers and sauté for another 10 minutes. Add meat to vegetables, bay leaves, thyme, mushrooms, potatoes and tomatoes. Add salt, pepper and Vegeta to taste. Add water to almost cover all ingredients, cover pot and slow simmer on low for 2 hours. Alternatively, you can cook in the oven for 2 hours on 350 degrees. Check meat to make sure it is tender and falling apart.

Serve with crusty bread.

Bean Stew with Smoked Pork

1 pound dried beans (any kind: kidney, romano, pinto)
12 cups of water
3 large onions, diced
2 celery stalks, finely diced
1 Tbsp Vegeta
5 bay leaves
Salt to taste
1 Tbsp ground pepper
1 tsp dried hot chili flakes
2 smoked pork hocks
½ cup oil
½ cup flour

In a large stock pot, cover beans with water and boil for 15 minutes. Drain water and add beans back to stock pot and add 12 cups of water. To the water, add 1/3 of the diced onions, celery, seasonings and bay leaves. Add pork hocks and add water if needed to cover all ingredients. Simmer on low for 1 ½ to 2 hours or until beans have doubled in size and are very soft.

In a frying pan, add oil and onions and sauté onions until golden and caramelized. Add flour to make a roux. Stir flour until combined well and flour starts to brown. Add the ground paprika and mix well. Take off the heat.

Slowly add roux; little by little to the beans and stir constantly to avoid lumps. Beans will start to thicken as you add roux. Stir until all the roux has been incorporated and bean stew has thickened. Add salt and pepper to taste. Remove pork hocks and shred meat into pieces and add back to stew and serve.

Fresh Green Pea Soup

1 large onion, finely chopped
2 celery stalks, finely chopped
1 parsnip, finely chopped
3 carrots, finely chopped
2 pounds frozen or fresh peas
½ cup fresh parsley, chopped
1 tsp black pepper
2 Tbsp Vegeta
16 cups of water
2-3 Tbsp oil

In a stock pot, add oil and onions and sauté on med-high for 10 minutes or until onions caramelize. Add celery, parsnip, and carrots and continue to sauté for 5 minutes, then add water and seasonings. Bring to a slow simmer, reduce to low and cook for 30 minutes. Add peas and cook for 5 minutes. Add parsley, adjust salt or Vegeta if needed and serve.

Chicken and Pea Stew

8 pieces of chicken, whole or any piece you like, skin removed.
2 large onions diced
1 carrot, diced
1 celery stalk, diced
2 Tbsp Vegeta
1 tsp pepper
1 tsp paprika
3 Tbsp cornstarch mixed with 4 Tbsp water
2 Tbsp water
2 pounds frozen or fresh peas
3 Tbsp oil

In a large pot, over medium-high heat, add oil and onions and sauté for 5 minutes. Add celery and carrots, sauté for 5 minutes. Add chicken and sauté on all sides until meat is light golden. Add water to just cover chicken, add spices and slow simmer for 30 minutes. Add peas and simmer for another 15 minutes. When done, combine cornstarch and 2 Tbsp water. Mix well and add to stew, stir fast until thickened.

Beef Goulash

2 pounds stewing beef, cut into 1 inch cubes
3 large onions, diced
2 cloves garlic, minced
1 cup tomato pureé
5 bay leaves
1 Tbsp dried thyme
2 Tbsp Vegeta
1 tsp hot dried chili flakes
1 tsp pepper
water
4 Tbsp oil
1 Tbsp paprika

Heat oil to med-high and brown beef on all sides. Remove from pan and set aside. In same pot, add onions and sauté until caramelized, for approximately 10-15 minutes. Add water, ¼ cup at a time, if the onions stick to the pan. Add all the herbs and spices and meat back into the pot with onions. Cover meat with water, just until meat is covered. Cover with lid and slow simmer for 2 hours. After 2 hours, add tomato pureé, check and add salt if needed. Continue to cook for 30 minutes or until meat is falling apart and tender. Serve over noodles or mashed potatoes.

Tomato and Pesto Soup

1 large onion, finely chopped
2 celery stalks, finely chopped
4 bay leaves
2 jars tomato passata (780 ml)
1 Tbsp Vegeta
1 tsp pepper
½ cup parsley, chopped
¼ cup olive oil
1 jar homemade or prepared pesto

In a large pot, add oil and sauté onions for 10 minutes until they start to turn golden. Add celery and bay leaves and sauté for 5 minutes. Add passata, seasonings and four jars of water (using passata jar). Bring to simmer, turn to low heat, cover and cook for 30 minutes. When done, stir in parsley and ladle soup into bowls. Top each bowl with 1 tsp pesto and serve.

Butternut Squash Soup

2 Tbsp oil
2 large onions, roughly chopped
2 large celery stalks, roughly chopped
2 roasted butternut squash, flesh scooped out
1-2 Tbsp Vegeta (or salt)
1 Tbsp ground cumin
1 tsp cinnamon
1 tsp ground black pepper
1 Tbsp curry paste
8 cups water
1 cup sour cream
1 cup chopped parsley

Sauté onions in oil for 5 minutes on high heat. Add celery and spices and stir together. Add squash and stir. Add water and stir. Bring to a simmer, then lower temperature. Simmer for approximately 30 minutes, or until vegetables are soft. Remove from heat. Using an immersion blender, blend until everything is smooth and silky. Add 1 cup tempered sour cream (see Tips and Tricks section). Add parsley. Stir.

Salads

Tuna and Avocado Salad

1 head Romaine lettuce, chopped
3 green onions, sliced
1 avocado, diced
3 mini cucumbers, sliced
1 can tuna in water
½ cup olive oil
¼ cup fresh lemon juice
1 Tbsp honey
1 tsp Dijon mustard
1 tsp salt
½ tsp black pepper

Combine lettuce, onions, avocado and cucumber. Combine oil, honey, mustard, salt, pepper and lemon juice. Mix well and pour over salad and toss. Place salad on a serving tray and top with tuna pieces evenly.

Moroccan Quinoa Salad

2 cups quinoa (cook according to instructions on package)
1 can white beans
1 cup shredded carrots
1 cup green onion, thinly sliced
1 cup cranberries, apricots or currents
2 Tbsp cumin
2 Tbsp ground coriander seed
1 cup sunflower seeds
1 cup fresh coriander
2 Tbsp pepper
2 tsp salt
1 tsp paprika
½ cup olive oil
¼ cup white balsamic vinegar

Mix all ingredients together and mix well until everything is coated evenly.

Rainbow Vegetable Salad

5 large kale leaves, finely chopped
1 carrot, peeled into ribbons
1 small fennel, sliced
1 bell pepper, thinly sliced
1 cup fresh coriander, chopped
1 pound sugar snap peas, sliced in half lengthwise
1 cup purple cabbage, shredded
1 red onion, thinly sliced
¼ of Daikon radish, sliced into ribbons
1 Tbsp salt
1 Tbsp pepper
1 Tbsp Dijon mustard
1 Tbsp jam (any kind)
¾ cup canola oil
½ cup apple cider vinegar

Put all vegetables in a large salad bowl and drizzle with dressing and toss. For the dressing combine salt, pepper, mustard, jam, oil and vinegar. Mix well.

Spinach and Watermelon Salad with Feta

1 large watermelon, cut into pieces or scooped out of shell
½ cup feta cheese, crumbled
1 cup fresh baby spinach
2 Tbsp olive oil
1 Tbsp balsamic glaze
1 tsp salt
1 tsp pepper

On a serving tray, layer spinach on the bottom, then place watermelon on top. Sprinkle everything with salt, pepper and crumbled feta. Drizzle oil and balsamic glaze evenly over spinach and watermelon.

Chicken and Mango Salad

1 cooked chicken breast sliced (leftovers or whole rotisserie chicken)
2 cups fresh baby spinach
1 mango, sliced
½ red onion, thinly sliced
¼ cup fresh coriander, chopped

Dressing:
½ cup canola oil
¼ cup white balsamic vinegar
½ tsp salt
½ tsp black pepper

Combine spinach, mango, onion and coriander in a salad bowl. Combine oil, vinegar, salt and pepper to make dressing and top on salad. Add chicken on top and serve.

Fennel and Orange Salad

1 bulb fennel, cut in half and thinly sliced
1 Vidalia onion, thinly sliced
4 sprigs fresh parsley, chopped
4 frons of fennel
1 navel orange, cut into segments
3 Tbsp olive oil
Juice of 1 orange
1 Tbsp white balsamic vinegar
Salt and pepper to taste

Layer sliced fennel, onions and oranges. Top with parsley and fennel frons. Combine oil, orange juice and vinegar. Spoon over salad and sprinkle with salt and pepper to taste.

Tropical Slaw

½ small head read cabbage, shredded
2 mangoes, thinly sliced
1 red pepper, thinly sliced
5 spring onions, thinly sliced
½ cup fresh cilantro, chopped

Dressing:
Juice of 1 lemon
1 Tbsp honey
½ cup olive oil
Salt and pepper to taste

Combine all vegetables together and drizzle with dressing. Toss until well combined.

Grilled Vegetable Salad

1 eggplant sliced into ½ inch slices (across)
4 zucchini sliced into ½ inch slices (lengthwise)
1 pound of 15-20 whole mushrooms
1 bunch green onions
½ cup olive oil
¼ cup balsamic vinegar
Salt and pepper to taste
2 cloves garlic, minced
½ cup goat cheese, crumbled

Grill all vegetables until grill marks on both sides. On a large serving platter, arrange grilled vegetables, slightly layering each group of vegetables or in any fashion you like. Mix together garlic, oil, vinegar, salt, pepper and evenly drizzle over vegetables. Crumble goat cheese on top and serve warm or chilled.

Mediterranean Pasta Salad

1 box cooked pasta (shells or penne)
5 green onions, thinly sliced
1-2 cloves garlic, minced
½ red onion, finely diced
½ cup black olives, pitted, diced
½ cup green olives, pitted, diced
¼ cup chopped fresh basil
¼ cup chopped fresh oregano
½ cup crumbled goat cheese
½ cup toasted pine nuts
½ cup chopped sundried tomatoes
¼ cup balsamic vinegar
½ cup olive oil

Combine all ingredients and add salt and pepper to taste.

Seafood Salad

1 pound, cooked medium sized shrimp
1 ¼ cup crab meat (imitation style)
1 yellow bell pepper, finely diced
1 small to medium purple onion, finely diced
4 green onions, thinly sliced
1 celery stalk, finely diced
1 cup fresh parsley, chopped
Juice of 1-2 lemons
4 Tbsp olive oil
Salt to taste
1 tsp pepper

Mix all ingredients together. Add lemon juice according to taste and size of lemons.

Potato and Dill Salad

3 pounds baby red potatoes
1 small red onion, finely diced
3 green onions, thinly sliced
1 cup fresh dill, chopped
½ cup canola oil
¼ cup white wine vinegar
1 Tbsp whole grain mustard
1 tsp salt
1 tsp pepper

Boil whole baby potatoes, with skins on until fork tender. Drain water and let cool for 30 minutes. When cool, cut potatoes in half and place in large salad bowl. Add both onions and dill. To make dressing, in a bowl, combine mustard, vinegar, oil, salt and pepper. Whisk until emulsified. Pour over potatoes and toss well until all potatoes are dressed.

Pear, Goat Cheese and Arugula Salad

1 head Romaine—chopped
1 bunch Arugula
½ vidalia onion, thinly sliced
1 bosc pear—cored and thinly sliced
½ cup roasted sunflower seeds
½ cup goat cheese, crumbled
pea shoots

Dressing
½ cup olive oil
¼ cup balsamic vinegar
½ tsp salt
1 tsp honey
1 tsp dijon mustard
¼ tsp pepper

On a serving plate layer the following ingredients: romaine, arugula, pears, onions, goat cheese, and sunflower seeds. Dress salad with dressing and add pea shoots as garnish on top, if desired.

Golden Beet and Citrus Salad

5 golden beets
1 orange
½ red onion, very thinly sliced
4 Tbsp olive oil
2 Tbsp white balsamic vinegar
½ tsp salt
½ tsp ground pepper

Place beets into a stockpot and add water to cover. Simmer until beets are fork tender, about 45 minutes. Remove beets, cool, peel and thinly slice. On a serving tray, arrange beets, top with oranges, onions and drizzle with oil and vinegar, sprinkle with salt and pepper.

Creamy Cucumber and Carrot Salad

5 mini English cucumbers, sliced
1 carrot, shredded
½ vidalia onion, finely diced
¼ cup fresh parsley, chopped
1 cup sour cream
½ tsp salt
½ tsp pepper

Combine all ingredients together, stir and serve.

Carrot and Cabbage Slaw

1 small head of cabbage, finely shredded
2 carrots, shredded
¼ cup fresh cilantro, chopped
½ cup sunflower oil
¼ cup white wine vinegar
1 tsp salt
1 tsp pepper
1 Tbsp white sugar

Combine all ingredients together and toss very well until all cabbage is dressed evenly.

Asian Noodle Salad

1 package rice vermicelli noodles, prepared according to package instructions
1 red bell pepper, thinly sliced
1 large carrot, shredded
¼ head of cabbage, thinly sliced
4 green onions, sliced
2 cups bean sprouts
½ cup fresh coriander

Dressing:
2 Tbsp hoisin sauce
1 Tbsp soy sauce
1 Tbsp fish sauce
2 Tbsp rice wine vinegar
2 Tbsp peanut butter
3 cloves minced garlic
1 Tbsp minced fresh ginger
1 Tbsp sriracha sauce
¼ cup sunflower oil

Combine all vegetables with noodles. Mix all dressing ingredients together and add to salad. Toss until well dressed.

Tomato, Arugula and Feta Salad

1 pound grape tomatoes, cut in half
4 cups baby arugula
1 cup feta, crumbled
1 vidalia onion, finely diced

Dressing:
½ cup olive oil
1 Tbsp balsamic glaze
1 tsp salt
½ tsp pepper

Combine tomatoes, arugula, onions and feta, drizzle dressing over top and mix until everything is combined.

Roasted Corn and Edamame Salad

1 bag frozen edamame
1 onion, chopped
1 can of lentils (540 ml), rinsed and drained
1 red pepper, chopped
2 bunch of parsley, chopped
6 cobs of roasted corn, kernels sliced off
1 tsp black ground pepper
1 tsp salt
¼ cup white balsamic vinegar
½ cup olive oil

Blanch frozen edamame in hot water for 1 minute. Rinse under cold water and drain. Add edamame, onion, lentils, red pepper, parsley and corn to a large bowl. Stir to combine. Add pepper, salt, balsamic vinegar and oil. Mix together.

Kale and Beet Salad with Feta

2 pounds beets, cooked and sliced
2 large garlic cloves, minced
¼ cup fresh cilantro, chopped
1 cup feta cheese, crumbled
2 tsp salt
1 tsp pepper
½ cup white balsamic vinegar
1 cup sunflower or vegetable oil

Simmer the beets, whole and unpeeled, in a large stock pot, covered with water, until beets are fork tender. Cool beets down, peel and thinly slice. Add all other ingredients. Mix well until all beets are well seasoned. If required, add another tsp of salt as beets can be sweet. Season to your taste.

Panzanella Salad

6 vine ripe tomatoes, diced
1 vidalia onion, thinly sliced
½ cup olive oil
1 tsp salt
½ tsp black pepper
2 cups croutons or baked pita chips

Combine all ingredients and mix well. Croutons will absorb all juices and soften. Make 30 minutes before serving.

One Pot Meals

Lentil Curry
Paella
Mexican Rice Casserole
Oyster Mushroom Risotto
Spinach and Feta Frittata
Prosciutto and Arugula Tart
Beef and Potato Moussaka
Potato and Sausage Casserole
Sauerkraut with Smoked Sausages
Fast Pita Bread Pizza

Lentil Curry

1 large onion, diced
3 Tbsp Indian curry paste
2 cups orange lentils
6 diced Roma tomatoes
4 cups water
½ cup fresh cilantro, chopped
3 Tbsp oil

In a large stockpot, add oil and onions. Sauté for 5 minutes. Add curry paste and sauté for a few minutes to cook out spices. Add tomatoes and lentils and stir until combined. Add water and bring to simmer. Turn down heat to low, cover and cook for 25-30 minutes or until liquid is absorbed and lentils are very soft. Add fresh cilantro and serve over cooked basmati rice.

Paella

3 Tbsp olive oil
2 large onions, diced
2 red bell peppers, finely diced
2 celery ribs, very finely diced
4 cloves garlic, minced
4 bay leaves
4 tomatoes, diced
2 chorizo sausages sliced
2 Tbsp Vegeta
1 Tbsp pepper
1 pound raw shelled shrimp
1 pound mussels
2 cups rice, traditionally bomba rice is used, I like white long grain rice.
3 cups water

In a sauté pan add oil, onion and bay leaves and sauté for 5 minutes. Add garlic, celery, peppers and sausage and sauté for another 5 mins. Add tomatoes and sauté for another 5 minutes. Season with Vegeta and pepper. In a large deep roasting pan, transfer the onion sausage sauté and add rice, water, shrimp and mussels evenly in pan. Bake in a 375 degree oven for approximately 30-40 minutes. Mussels will have opened and rice will be tender with all liquid absorbed.

Mexican Rice Casserole

1 pound ground beef
2 onions, diced
1 red pepper, diced
3 tomatoes, diced
1 can corn
1 can black beans
2 Tbsp ground cumin
1 Tbsp black pepper
1 Tbsp paprika
1 Tbsp garlic powder
1 Tbsp dried oregano
2 Tbsp Vegeta
2 cups long grain rice
3 Tbsp oil
4 cups water
½ cup fresh cilantro

In a deep skillet, sauté onion and peppers for 5 minutes in oil. Add beef and sauté until no longer pink. Add tomatoes, corn, black beans and spices. Stir until combined. Add rice and 4 cups of water. Cook on low, with lid on, until rice is done. Sprinkle with chopped cilantro and serve.

Oyster Mushroom Risotto

1 large onion, finely diced
1 pound oyster mushrooms, whole
1 cup Arborio rice
5 cups hot chicken stock
1 Tbsp Vegeta
1 tsp pepper
2 Tbsp butter
1 cup Parmigiano Reggiano cheese
2 Tbsp oil

In oil, sauté onions for 5 minutes. Add mushrooms and sauté for 7 minutes. Add rice and coat rice with mushrooms. Add 1 cup of stock and stir until almost all is absorbed. Then add remainder of stock and keep repeating until rice is cooked, but still al dente in the centre. Once done, remove from heat and add butter and cheese. Stir until melted and blended.

Spinach and Feta Frittata

12 eggs
5 green onions, sliced thinly
1 pound baby spinach
1 cup feta, crumbled
1 tsp Vegeta
1 tsp salt
1 tsp pepper
3 Tbsp butter
2 tomatoes, sliced thinly

In a large oven proof sauté pan, add butter and onions and sauté for 3-5 minutes. Beat egg lightly, season with salt and pepper and pour into pan with sautéed onions. Add spinach and stir until everything is evenly combined with eggs. Place the pan in a 350 degree pre-heated oven and bake for 15 minutes or until eggs are set. Slice and serve.

Prosciutto and Arugula Tart

1 package store bought puff pastry
½ cup ricotta cheese
6 slices prosciutto
handful of arugala
½ tsp salt
½ tsp pepper
4 fresh basil leaves, chopped
1 Tbsp olive oil
1 Tbsp balsamic glaze

Roll out puffed pastry on a baking sheet and bake according to package instructions for approximately 20 minutes or until golden brown. Place puffed pastry on a board or platter. Mix ricotta, salt, pepper and basil and spread evenly onto cooked puffed pastry. Place prosciutto evenly on pastry. Scatter arugula and drizzle evenly with olive oil and balsamic glaze. Lightly salt arugula according to taste. Top off with 2-3 shaved pieces of Parmesan cheese.

Beef and Potato Moussaka

8–10 potatoes, sliced into ¼ inch slices
2 onions
1 pound ground beef
1 Tbsp Vegeta
1 tsp pepper
1 tsp paprika
1 tsp dried thyme
3 Tbsp oil
2 eggs
1 cup sour cream
¼ cup parsley, chopped

In oil, sauté onions for 10 minutes until translucent and golden. Add beef and sauté for 10-15 minutes or until beef is cooked through. Add spices. In a large baking dish, layer potatoes and overlap a little bit on the side evenly, covering ¼ of each slice. Pour meat mixture over potato layer and cover with second layer of potatoes. Pour 1 cup water over potatoes, and bake at 350 degrees for 60 minutes or until potatoes are fork tender. Remove and whisk eggs together with sour cream and parsley and pour over potatoes, return in oven and bake for 10 minutes, uncovered.

Potato and Sausage Casserole

8 yellow flesh potatoes cut into ½ inch slices
2 red bell peppers, diced
2 onions, diced
5 roma tomatoes, diced
1 cup long grain rice
6 sausages (Italian or smoked)
4 bay leaves
1 Tbsp dried thyme
2 Tbsp Vegeta
1 Tbsp black pepper
3 cups water

In a roasting pan, add all ingredients, except sausage, and combine well.

Place sausages on top and bake at 350 degrees for 60 minutes. Turn sausages over after first 30 minutes and brown on both sides. If all water evaporates, add more water.

Sauerkraut with Smoked Sausages

2 jars shredded sauerkraut
4 onions, sliced thinly
5 bay leaves
Ground pepper to taste
4 smoked sausages, sliced into 1 inch pieces

In a deep roasting pan, add sauerkraut and all other ingredients. Combine and distribute meat evenly. Cover with one jar of water and bake at 350 degrees for 2-2 ½ hours or until the sauerkraut is soft. Add water throughout cooking to keep moist on bottom, but not to cover the ingredients.

Fast Pita Bread Pizza

Greek or Turkish Style pita bread
1 tomato, thinly sliced
5 fresh basil leaves or 1 tsp dried basil
Ricotta cheese
Olive oil

Preheat oven to 425 degrees.

On a pita bread, drizzle olive oil and evenly spread with fingers or brush. Top with tomatoes, herbs and cheese. Sprinkle with salt and pepper to taste. Drizzle with olive oil again and bake for 5-7 minutes or until cheese is melted and bubbly.

You can always use fresh dough, but this is something I do when everyone is hungry and needs a quick meal or when you need to whip up a fast appetizer when guests arrive.

Pasta

Creamy Mushroom Pasta
Baked French Onion Gnocchi
Creamy Feta Cheese Pasta
Butternut Squash and Spinach Pasta
Creamy Chicken and Spinach Pasta
Pear, Hazelnut and Gorgonzola Pasta
Tomato and Meat Sauce with Pasta
Pumpkin Pasta
Kale and Pesto Pasta
Baked Stuffed Crepes
Brussel Sprout and Hazelnut Fettuccini

Creamy Mushroom Pasta

1 large onion, finely diced
3 garlic cloves, minced
1 pound whole mushrooms, sliced
5 sage leaves fresh, finely sliced
2 Tbsp flour
3 cups water
1 cup sour cream
1 tsp salt
1 tsp Vegeta
3 Tbsp oil
1 package of pasta (ex: penne, rigatoni, farfalle)

Heat oil and sauté onions and garlic for 5 minutes. Add mushrooms, salt, Vegeta, and pepper and cook for 10 minutes. Sprinkle flour over mushrooms and mix well until blended. Add water and stir until the sauce thickens. Once the sauce is thick, take pan off heat and add sour cream. Stir until blended. Pour over cooked pasta.

Baked French Onion Gnocchi

3 large onions, very thinly sliced
5 sage leaves fresh, sliced
2 Tbsp butter
2 Tbsp oil
3 Tbsp flour
2 cups beef broth
3 cups old cheddar cheese, grated
1 tsp Vegeta
1 tsp black pepper
2 pounds frozen gnocchi, prepared according to package instructions

In saucepan, combine butter, oil and onions. Sauté for 20 minutes until onions are caramelized. Deglaze with ¼ cup water as needed. Add flour and mix well. Add broth and stir until smooth and mixture thickens. Season with Vegeta and pepper and add 2 cups of cheese. Add cooked gnocchi and stir. Pour mixture in large baking pan, top with 1 cup cheese and bake at 400 degrees for 20 minutes. Cheese will be melted and golden.

Creamy Feta Cheese Pasta

2 cups sour cream
1 cup feta cheese, crumbled
½ cup fresh parsley, chopped
4 green onions, finely sliced
1 Tbsp fresh or dried oregano
1 box/package of pasta

Cook pasta according to instructions. Combine all ingredients into cooked pasta. Stir well and serve.

Fast, easy and impressive.

Butternut Squash and Spinach Pasta

2 garlic cloves, minced
3 Tbsp olive oil
1 Tbsp butter
3 sage leaves
2 pounds butternut squash, diced
1 onion, finely diced
1 cup chicken or vegetable broth
1 box/package pasta
2 cups spinach
1 tsp Vegeta
1 tsp pepper
¼ cup parmigiano reggiano cheese

In a large pan, add oil, butter and sage leaves. Cook for 1 minute and remove leaves. In the same oil, add onions and cook for 5 minutes. Add squash and sauté. Add broth little by little and simmer for approximately 15-20 minutes or until squash is soft and cooked. Add spinach, Vegeta and pepper and sauté until wilted. Add cooked pasta and cheese and serve hot.

Creamy Chicken and Spinach Pasta

1 pound dry pasta, cook according to package directions
2 boneless/skinless chicken breasts, cut into 1 inch cubes
3 Tbsp olive oil
3 cloves garlic, minced
1 package of spinach, frozen
1 cup sundried tomatoes in oil, chopped
2 tsp Vegeta
1 tsp pepper
1 tsp dried oregano
1 cup cream cheese
1 cup water
½ cup parmigiano reggiano cheese

Sauté chicken in oil until cooked through, approximately 10 minutes. Add garlic, spinach, sundried tomatoes and all spices and sauté for another 5-6 mins. Add cream cheese and water and bring to a simmer and cook for 2 minutes, until sauce comes together with all ingredients. Add cooked pasta to the pan and toss, add parmigiano reggiano cheese and serve.

Pear, Hazelnut and Gorgonzola Pasta

1 pound pasta, cooked according to package instructions
2 pears diced
2 Tbsp olive oil
2 Tbsp butter
1 tsp fresh thyme
1 cup sour cream
1 cup ricotta cheese
1 tsp salt
½ tsp pepper
½ cup gorgonzola cheese, crumbled
½ cup pasta cooking water
1 cup roasted hazelnuts, chopped roughly

Sauté pears and thyme in oil and butter for 3-5 minutes. Add sour cream, ricotta cheese, gorgonzola cheese and pasta water. Bring to a simmer and stir until a smooth sauce forms and reduces a little bit. Season with salt and pepper, add cooked pasta to pan and toss until sauce coats pasta. Sprinkle with hazelnuts and serve.

Tomato and Meat Sauce with Pasta

1 onion, diced
3 cloves garlic, minced
1 pound ground beef
1 Tbsp dried oregano
¼ cup fresh basil leaves
1 tsp salt
1 tsp pepper
1 L crushed tomatoes
2 Tbsp olive oil

Sauté garlic, onions and beef in oil until beef is no longer pink (approximately 10 minutes). Add oregano, basil and tomatoes. Reduce to low heat. Cover with lid and simmer for 1 ½ hours. This is a basic meat sauce that can be served over pasta or used in a lasagna dish.

Pumpkin Pasta

2 large onions, chopped
2 Tbsp oil
1 large can pure pumpkin purée
1 cup milk
½ cup cream
1 Tbsp Vegeta (or salt)
1 tsp black pepper
1 cup fresh parsley, chopped
1 cup parmigiano reggiano cheese, grated finely

Sauté onions in oil until lightly golden. Add pumpkin purée and stir. Next, mix in milk and cream. Finally, add Vegeta (or salt), pepper and chopped parsley. Stir until combined. Cook on a slow simmer for a few minutes. Add sauce to cooked pasta and top with cheese.

Kale and Pesto Pasta

2 onions, diced
1 bunch of kale, finely chopped
1 box or bag of pasta, prepared according to directions and drained
3 Tbsp olive oil
3 Tbsp pesto
½ lemon (juice)
salt (to taste)
pepper (to taste)

In oil, sauté onions until golden. Add kale and sauté for 5 minutes or until wilted and cooked. Add pesto, lemon juice, salt and pepper and drained pasta. Toss and serve. Sprinkle with Parmesan cheese on top, if desired.

Baked Stuffed Crepes

4 eggs
¼ tsp salt
3 cups flour
1 tsp sugar
2 cups water
2 cups milk

Make crepes: Beat eggs, add salt, sugar and flour. Slowly add water/milk liquid as you whisk until smooth. You need a runny consistency. Add more water as needed. Grease heated pan. Cook crepes on medium-high heat. Gently flip over. Re-grease after 3-4 crepes.

Filling:
1 cup feta, crumbled
2 eggs
2 cups ricotta cheese
1 tsp salt

Mix together filling ingredients. Fill and roll each crepe like a log and then roll into a circle/coil. Place double rolled crepes in a baking pan. Make an egg wash with 1 egg and 1 Tbsp milk. Brush rolled crepes with egg wash. Bake in 350 degree oven for 20 minutes or until browned and bubbly.

Brussel Sprouts and Hazelnut Fettuccini

1 pound Brussel sprouts, quartered
1 onion, sliced thin
2 garlic cloves, minced
5 sage leaves, thinly sliced
½ cup butter
1 box, dried pasta, cooked
1 cup hazelnuts, toasted and chopped
½ cup parmigiano reggiano

In a saucepan, melt butter, heat over medium/high heat and add onions. Sauté until onions start to brown. Add garlic, sage and brussel sprouts. Continue and sauté for 10 minutes or until brussel sprouts are fork tender. Add pasta and ½ cup pasta water. Stir well. Top with hazelnuts and cheese. Serve.

Meat and Fish

Grilled Chicken Kebabs
Mediterranean Turkey Meatballs
Pulled Pork
Miso Glazed Salmon
Beef Rib Ragu with Egg Noodles
Roasted Pork Tenderloin
Turkish Eggplant with Beef
Serbian Style Pork Burgers
Sticky Garlic Chicken
Beef Stuffed Peppers
Roasted Lemon and Herb Salmon Filet
Dried Fruit and Feta Stuffed Pork Loin
Mediterranean Mussels
Super Moist Meatloaf
Oven Roasted Chicken

Grilled Chicken Kebabs

1 lb chicken breasts, 1 inch cubes
2 garlic cloves, minced
1 lemon, juiced
½ cup olive oil
2 tsp dried oregano
1 tsp salt
1 tsp black pepper

In a bowl, add all ingredients and marinate in fridge for 2-24 hours. When done, add 3-4 pieces on skewers and grill on medium to high heat for 3-4 minutes per side. Serve with yogurt and fresh parsley.

Mediterranean Turkey Meatballs

1 lb ground turkey
1 cup feta cheese, crumbled
½ cup sundried tomatoes in oil, chopped
1 tsp Vegeta
1 tsp black pepper
1 tsp dried oregano
1 cup drained and thawed frozen spinach
2 garlic cloves, minced

Mix all ingredients together and form into 1 inch balls.

In 3 Tbsp canola oil, fry balls on all sides for 3-4 minutes. Serve in a pita bread with a dollop of yogurt.

Pulled Pork

3-4 lbs pork shoulder
1 Tbsp Vegeta
1 Tbsp ground cumin
1 Tbsp chili powder
1 Tbsp garlic powder
1 Tbsp dried oregano
1 tsp cinnamon
1 tsp smoked paprika
1 tsp black pepper
1 cup smokey BBQ sauce

Combine all spices together and rub onto meat evenly. Place meat in covered roasting pan and add water to cover half way up the meat. Bake covered at 350 degrees for 3 hours.

Remove pork from pan and pull meat apart with hands or two forks. Mix meat in with roasting liquid, add BBQ sauce and mix well.

Miso Glazed Salmon

1 whole salmon filet
1 tsp Miso
2 Tbsp honey
2 garlic cloves, minced
1 tsp fresh ginger, grated

Place salmon on foil lined baking sheet. Mix all ingredients together and spoon evenly over salmon. Bake at 450 degrees for 10 minutes.

Braised Beef Ragu with Egg Noodles

2 cloves garlic, minced
2 onions, diced
2 carrots, diced
2 celery stalks, diced
3 lbs beef ribs
4 bay leaves
1 tsp thyme
1 L tomato passata
1 L water
2 Tbsp oil
1 package pasta, cooked

Add oil to sauté pan and brown ribs on both sides and remove. In the same pan with beef drippings, add onions, carrots, celery, bay leaves and thyme and sauté for 10 mins, deglaze with ¼ cup of water, if needed. Add passata, water and ribs. Simmer on low heat for 1.5 hrs or until ribs are tender. When done, remove ribs and pull meat off the bone and cut into small pieces. Add meat back to sauce. Stir and serve over cooked noodles and top with parmesan cheese.

Roasted Pork Tenderloin

2 whole pork tenderloins
1 tsp salt
1 tsp pepper
1 tsp smoked paprika
1 Tbsp oil

Stir spices and oil together and rub on tenderloins. Roast in a pre-heated oven (350 degrees) for 35 minutes or until cooked.

Turkish Eggplant with Beef

2 medium eggplants, sliced into 1 inch pieces
3 cloves garlic, minced
3 Tbsp oil

1 lb ground beef
1 onion, diced
2 cloves garlic, minced
1 tsp Vegeta
1 tsp ground cumin
1 tsp black pepper
½ tsp cinnamon
1 tsp paprika
¼ cup fresh parsley, chopped
3 Tbsp oil

Place sliced eggplant on baking sheet, brush with oil on one side. Sprinkle with garlic and bake at 400 degrees for 30 minutes or until golden.

In a skillet, add oil, onions and sauté for 5 minutes. Add garlic and beef. Sauté until brown. Add spices and parsley. Sauté for another 5-7 minutes.

Top meat mixture on eggplant slices and serve with a dollop of sour cream or greek yogurt.

Serbian Style Pork Burgers (Serbian Pjeskavice)

1 ½ pounds ground pork
½ pound ground beef
½ Tbsp salt
1 tsp black pepper
½ tsp or to taste hot pepper flakes
1 tsp paprika
¼ tsp baking soda
2 large onions, very finely minced

Combine all ingredients and mix very well. Shape into very thin, larger burgers.

Cook on the BBQ.

Serve on Greek or Turkish style pita breads that have been grilled on the BBQ.

Top with sour cream or cream cheese and chopped sweet onions.

Sticky Garlic Chicken

1 whole chicken, cut into 8 pieces or any chicken parts you like (8-10 pieces)
3 cloves garlic, minced
2 inch piece of ginger, minced
½ cup soy sauce
2 Tbsp honey
¼ cup oil
2 Tbsp fish sauce
Juice of 1 lemon
½ cup chopped coriander

Place all meat in bowl. Combine all marinade ingredients and pour over chicken. Marinade for a minimum of four hours or preferably overnight.

Preheat oven to 350 degrees and evenly space out chicken onto a baking pan. Bake for 40-50 minutes or until dark golden and cooked through. Take leftover marinade and cook in sauce pan until reduced by half and has thickened. Once meat is done, remove onto serving dish and drizzle with sauce.

Beef Stuffed Peppers

1 pound ground beef
1 large onion, diced
1 Tbsp Vegeta
1 tsp pepper
1 tsp paprika
3 bay leaves
4-5 large red bell peppers
½ cup uncooked long grain rice
3 Tbsp oil

In oil, sauté onions for 10 minutes. Add beef and sauté until beef is no longer pink. Add all spices and seasoning and raw rice. Mix and set aside.

Core peppers and set in deep baking dish or roasting pan. Stuff meat mixture into peppers evenly. Add water to pan to cover peppers approximately one quarter of the way up.

Bake at 350 degrees for one hour.

Serve with 1 Tbsp of sour cream on top, if desired.

Roasted Lemon and Herb Salmon Filet

1 whole salmon filet
2 green onions, sliced
1 lemon, thinly sliced
¼ cup parsley, freshly chopped
2 Tbsp olive oil
Salt and pepper to taste

Pre-heat oven to 450 degrees. In a sheet pan, place fillet on parchment paper and season with salt and pepper. Top with lemon slices and dill. Drizzle with oil. Roast uncovered for 10 minutes. Remove and cut filets into 4 inch slices.

Dried Fruit and Feta Stuffed Pork Loin

1 Pork Loin Roast
1 cup feta cheese
⅓ cup prunes, pitted and chopped
⅓ cup dried apricots, chopped
⅓ cup dried figs, chopped

Sauce
1 cup red wine
1 tsp dried thyme
1 Tbsp butter
1 Tbsp honey

Butterfly pork loin and season both sides with salt and pepper. Mix together feta cheese and all dried fruit. Spread onto pork loin. Roll meat and tie with kitchen string. Place pork loin in roasting pan and place on the stove. Brown all sides of roast for 1-2 minutes. Transfer to oven and roast at 350 degrees for 60 minutes.

For sauce, simmer wine, thyme, butter, and honey for 5 minutes.

Slice roast and serve with sauce.

Mediterranean Mussels

2 lbs mussels, wash and remove the mussels that do not close.

Sauce
3 Tbsp olive oil
1 onion, finely diced
4 cloves garlic, minced
4 bay leaves
1 lb tomatoes, diced
1 Tbsp Vegeta
1 tsp pepper
1 cup chopped fresh parsley

Pour oil in a large stock pot and sauté onions, bay leaves and garlic for 5 minutes. Add tomatoes and sauté for another 5 minutes. Add mussels, stir to coat all mussels in sauce and cover with lid. Cook the mussels for 7 minutes, until all shells open. Add parsley and mix well to coat shells with sauce and parsley.

Super Moist Meatloaf

2 lbs ground beef
2 large onions, finely diced
1 celery stalk, finely diced
1 cup bread crumbs
1 cup milk
½ cup BBQ sauce for meatloaf
½ cup BBQ sauce for the top
1 egg
1 Tbsp Vegeta (or salt)
1 tsp black pepper
1 tsp smoked paprika

Combine all ingredients thoroughly.

Line large baking dish with parchment or foil.

Make two thin, flattened logs.

Bake 350 degrees 30-40 minutes, until meat is cooked.

Oven Roasted Chicken

Whole chicken
1 tsp paprika
1 tsp black pepper
1 tsp Vegeta
1 tsp salt

Mix spice mixture together. Rub onto whole chicken. Place chicken into roasting pan. Roast in a convection oven at 350 degrees for 1 hour or regular oven at 350 degrees for 1 hour 15 minutes or until golden brown and juices run clear.

Side Dishes

Garlic Sautéed Mushrooms
Garlic Rapini
Roasted Tomato and Pepper Confit (Bechar Paprikash)
Garlic Green Beans
Cornbread with Feta Cheese
Roasted Root Vegetables
Caramelized Onion Mashed Potatoes
Baked Peppers Stuffed with Cheese
Stuffed Roasted Onions
Oven Roasted Mixed Vegetables
Whole Roasted Cauliflower
Roasted Potatoes with Sriracha Aioli
Grilled Asparagus
Creamed Spinach
Smashed Potatoes with Kale and Goat Cheese
Balsamic and Garlic Roasted Eggplant
Freshly Baked Bread

Garlic Sautéed Mushrooms

1 pound white button mushrooms, whole
4 Tbsp butter
1 tsp salt
1 tsp black pepper
¼ cup fresh parsley, chopped
½ cup water

Place butter and garlic in a large skillet with a lid. Let butter melt evenly and stir in garlic. Place mushrooms, cap side down, cover with lid and place on medium-high heat for 3 minutes. Add water and close lid to steam mushrooms for another 2-3 minutes. Stir mushrooms until all pieces come off of the bottom of the pan. Season and add parsley. Transfer to a serving bowl.

Garlic Rapini

1 bunch of rapini or 1 pound
3 Tbsp olive oil
3 garlic cloves, finely chopped
Salt to taste

Wash and cut stems from the leafy tops of the rapini. In a large stock pot, add 1 cup water and add stems and then leafy tops on top layer. Bring to a high boil and steam rapini for 2 minutes or until wilted. Place rapini onto baking sheet and spread out evenly. Drizzle with olive oil and garlic and sprinkle with salt. Bake in preheated oven at 400 degrees for 7 minutes, until tender, but not overcooked. Serve.

Roasted Tomato and Pepper Confit (Bechar Paprikash)

4 large onions, diced
15 large red bell peppers, diced
9 large Roma tomatoes, diced
1 Tbsp Vegeta
1 tsp pepper
1 cup fresh chopped parsley
½ cup oil

In a large roasting pan. add peppers, onions, tomatoes, oil and spices and roast uncovered in oven at 350 degrees for 90 mins. Make sure to stir every 30 mins. Juices will evaporate and concentrate. When done add parsley, stir and serve.

Serve as a side dish or in an omelette or with a fried egg on top.

Garlic Green Beans

1 pound French green beans
2 cloves garlic, minced
½ stick of butter (¼ cup)
Salt and pepper to taste
Handful chopped fresh parsley

In a deep frying pan, on high heat, melt butter and add garlic and beans. Sauté beans to coat with butter. Add ½ cup water and cover with lid. This will create steam. Remove lid after 5 minutes or when water evaporates. Add salt, pepper and parsley. Stir and serve.

Corn Bread with Feta Cheese

3 eggs, beaten
1 cup water
1 cup buttermilk
1 cup oil
1 ½ cup corn meal
1 ½ cup flour
1 tsp baking powder
1 tsp salt
½ tsp pepper
1 cup feta cheese, crumbled

Mix all wet ingredients together, then add all dry ingredients. At the end, sprinkle in the feta cheese and fold ingredients together. Bake at 350 degrees for 35 minutes or until light golden and insert toothpick until it comes out clean.

Roasted Root Vegetables

2 parsnips
5 carrots (baby or heirloom, whole or half)
1 rutabaga, largely diced
2 onions, cut into pieces
3 sweet potatoes, diced
3 Tbsp olive oil
3 Tbsp dried thyme
1 Tbsp ground pepper
Salt to taste
3 garlic cloves, minced

Cut and coat all vegetables with oil and spices. Spread out evenly onto large baking sheet and bake at 400 degrees for 45 minutes until soft and golden brown.

Caramelized Onion Mashed Potatoes

8 potatoes, peeled and cubed
2 large onions, finely diced
4 Tbsp oil
1 Tbsp oil
1 tsp Vegeta
1 tsp pepper
1 tsp paprika

In a large stockpot, cover potatoes with water and simmer until fork tender. Drain, mash and set aside. In a fry pan, sauté onions in oil for 15 minutes or until onions are golden and caramelized. If onions stick to pan, add ¼ cup water and keep sautéing until done. Add caramelized onion mixture to mashed potatoes and add spices. Mix onion mixture into potatoes and serve.

Baked Peppers Stuffed with Cheese

6 red bell peppers
1 ¼ cup feta cheese
1 cup cottage cheese
3 eggs
1 tsp salt
1 tsp pepper
1 Tbsp oil

Trim the tops of peppers and expose the hole. Brush oil all over the outside of each pepper. Stuff peppers with cheese filling. For filling, mix all cheese, eggs, salt and pepper. Stuff peppers and bake at 400 degrees for 30-40 minutes or until peppers blister and char.

Stuffed Roasted Onions

6 large red onions
3 slices of pancetta
1 cup Shredded Gouda or White Cheddar cheese
1 cup cooked rice
1 tsp Vegeta
1 tsp pepper
¼ cup fresh parsley, chopped

Cut onions across in halves. Take out the centers leaving about an inch of onion as the base. Finely chop the onion centers and sauté with pancetta until pancetta is crisp and onions are soft and golden (approximately 10 minutes). Add rice and Vegeta and pepper.

Fill the onion circles with the pancetta mix and bake in a 400-degree oven for 15 minutes. Remove from oven and add shredded Gouda cheese to each onion and bake for another 5 minutes.

Oven Roasted Mixed Vegetables

1 pound whole green beans, trimmed
1 pound whole button mushrooms
red, yellow and orange peppers, sliced
¼ cup oil
1 Tbsp garlic powder
1 tsp dried thyme
1 tsp black pepper
1 tsp salt

Wash and prepare vegetables. Leave beans and mushrooms whole and slice peppers. Mix oil and seasonings together with vegetables. In a large roasting pan, roast vegetables at 400 degrees for 15-20 minutes.

Whole Roasted Cauliflower

1 whole cauliflower
1 Tbsp ground cumin
1 tsp turmeric
1 tsp black pepper
1 Tbsp paprika
2 Tbsp tahini
¼ cup olive oil
1 Tbsp Vegeta

Stir all spices and oil together and evenly coat the cauliflower head. Place on baking pan and bake at 350 degrees for one hour. When done, break apart the florets and serve with a dollop of green yogurt or a squeeze of fresh lemon.

Roasted Potatoes with Sriracha Aioli

6 Yukon gold potatoes, cubed
1 tsp salt
1 tsp black pepper
¼ cup oil
1 lime, juiced
½ cup mayonnaise
1 Tbsp sriracha sauce
2 Tbsp fresh cilantro, chopped

In a baking pan, add potatoes, oil, salt and pepper and roast at 400 degrees for 40-45 minutes or until soft and golden in colour. Place roasted potatoes on serving platter. Combine mayonnaise, sriracha, cilantro and lime juice and drizzle over potatoes.

Grilled Asparagus

1 bunch asparagus
3 Tbsp olive oil
1 Tbsp balsamic glaze
2 garlic cloves, minced
Salt and pepper to taste

Grill asparagus on BBQ or on stove top in a grill pan until marks show or 2 minutes per side. Place on a serving dish. In a bowl, mix garlic, oil and balsamic glaze. Drizzle on top of asparagus. Sprinkle with salt and pepper.

Creamed Spinach

1 package of frozen spinach, thawed and all liquid squeezed out
3 Tbsp garlic, minced
3 Tbsp flour
4 Tbsp oil
3 cups milk
1 Tbsp Vegeta
1 tsp black pepper

In oil, sauté garlic for 30 seconds and add flour to make a roux. Mix flour until blended and add milk, one cup at a time. Using whisk, stir consistently until thick and no lumps remain. Add Vegeta, pepper and spinach and mix until blended.

Smashed Roasted Potato with Kale and Goat Cheese

8 medium Yukon Gold potatoes
1 head kale, chopped finely
1 large onion, diced
2 garlic cloves, chopped
¼ cup canola oil
3 Tbsp oil
1 cup goat cheese
Salt and pepper to taste

Boil potatoes until soft. Place potatoes on a sheet pan and smash or flatten potatoes with spatula until 1 ½ inches thick. Drizzle all sides of potatoes with ½ cup oil and bake at 400 degrees for 30 minutes until golden. Season with salt and pepper to taste. In a sauté pan, add 3 Tbsp oil, onion and garlic and sauté for 5 minutes. Add kale and sauté for another 5-7 minutes. Season with salt and pepper. Add cheese and mix until combined. Place kale and cheese on top of roasted potatoes and enjoy.

Balsamic and Garlic Roasted Eggplant

4 baby eggplants, cut in half
2 garlic cloves, minced
¼ cup olive oil
1 Tbsp balsamic glaze
1 tsp salt
1 tsp black pepper
1 tsp dried oregano

Combine oil and garlic in a bowl and brush mixture over eggplant on cut sides. Place on a baking sheet cut side up, sprinkle with salt, pepper and oregano. Roast in oven at 400 degrees for 3 minutes or until soft and golden brown. Place eggplant on serving platter and drizzle balsamic glaze over eggplant.

Freshly Baked Bread

3 cups all purpose flour
2 cups water
2 tsp salt
1 tsp dry yeast

Mix all ingredients in a large mixing bowl until combined. The dough will look very dry and clumpy, do not worry as it will smooth out when rising. Cover bowl with plastic wrap and leave on the counter to rise for a minimum of 6 hours or overnight. When ready to bake, pre-heat both the oven and cast iron enamelled dutch oven pot to 450 degrees. Once the pot has pre-heated, place dough in pot and cover with lid, bake for 30 minutes. After 30 minutes remove lid and continue to bake for another 15 minutes. Once done remove from pot and cool on a rack.

We want to give a huge thank you to all the sponsors that made our book launch and this book possible.

Diamond Sponsors

Foxglove Design—The Foxglove Design Studio offers an opportunity for inspiration and a place to discuss style and design ideas. It is especially helpful for those thinking of custom building, renovating or redesigning a space with many samples in the studio to inspire and view. Come in to see our cabinet displays as well as our beautiful working kitchen. We love transforming spaces and working with our amazing clients to make their vision a reality! Let's start with a complimentary consultation at your home to discuss your project! 15140 Yonge Street, Unit 2 Aurora, ON L4G 1M2 289-466-1048 info.design@foxglovedesign.ca www.foxglovedesign.ca

Hola York Region—Hola York Region is an English/Spanish language magazine bringing you the latest in local news and lifestyle content with a Hispanic twist. Through engaging stories and information we celebrate and highlight Hispanic culture creating content that is timely and relevant to our multicultural readers across York Region. Contact information: Cindy Shaver and Chole Vargas 905-806-4737 info@holayorkregion.com www.holayorkregion.com 6-14845 Yonge Street, Suite 257, Aurora, ON, L4G 6H8

Manfred Gingl has been the Chief Executive Officer of BionX International, Aurora ON, since 2010. BionX, a producer of electric bike systems, is on a mission to revolutionize the way people move. The award-winning electric drive systems are answering a growing worldwide demand for alternative transportation solutions that enable environmental sustainability.Mr. Gingl has served as President and Chief Operating Officer of Magna from December 1981 as well as many other positions within the Magna corporation, Executive Vice Chairman of Magna Steyr AG & Co. KG, Chairman of Tesma International Inc and Cheif Executive Officer of Sancturary Day Spas.

Platinum Sponsors

Amanda Gobatto—Digital Girl Consulting—Training small business owners to have a successful and effective online presence for their brand is our passion. Our goal is to teach you how to market your business online by sharing your story, providing valuable and meaningful content for your followers and building/nurturing relationships with potential and new customers. Contact: Amanda Gobatto www.digitalgirlconsulting.com amanda@digitalgirlconsulting.com

Debra Wilson—Momentum Gold provides essential services such as energy (gas, electricity and solar), telecom, merchant services, security systems, wireless telecom and internet to both commercial and residential users. Momentum Gold operates in 25 countries and we would love the opportunity to help you with your services! www.momentumgold.acnibo.com

Russell Aquatics is a private swim school in Markham that has been offering the highest quality of swimming lessons for over a decade. At Russell Aquatics we aim to teach in an environment that is enthusiastic, safe & challenging for children to learn to swim. As of Spring 2018 we will open our very first custom built facility in East Markham. We look forward to seeing you at the pool! www.russellaquatics.com info@russellaquatics.com

Elizabeth Johnston—Currently President at The Business Women's Network of York Region, Director of the Lake Simcoe Championship Ice Fishing Derby, Business Partner of Canadian Tire Keswick & Petroleum, Owner of Thorah Garden Island Organic Farm, Owner of Trail of the Woods Bed & Breakfast and Owner of Kids Cash, a product to help teach children money management. Grew up in York Region, skied in Banff for 2 years, then lived in Australia for 15 years where she worked with the Dean of Commerce & Economics, The Small Business Development Corporation and her own marketing company Magnetic Data. Cell: 416-910-1058

Marilyn Harvey—Marilyn Harvey is a creative thinker who has a gift for moving retail projects forward. Assisting her clients to develop and define their vision, through to concept development, design, construction, merchandise procurement, human resource protocols

and the execution of the defined strategic plan. Marilyn delivers profitable turnkey results. http://www.luxuryretailspecialist.com marilyn@mh2.ca 1-403-678-7057 (cell)

Gold Sponsors

NewRoads Automotive Group has a long history in the automotive industry. It has been owned and operated by the Croxon family since 1968. The NewRoads Automotive family currently includes a group of five dealerships located in York Region- NewRoads Chevrolet Cadillac Buick GMC, NewRoads Subaru of Richmond Hill, NewRoads Mazda, NewRoads Chrysler Dodge Jeep Ram and NewRoads Subaru of Newmarket. NewRoads is dedicated to caring for our community through sponsorship and participation. Learn more about the NewRoads Automotive Group and for links to our social media visit http://www.newroads.ca

Angela Jones is an accomplished full time, full service Realtor who brings a strategic yet personal approach to the home buying and home selling process. Drawing from 19 years of award winning experience Angela has fine tuned her negotiating skills and proven her ability to guide buyers through a stress free and exciting purchase of their dream home to assisting sellers with her proven marketing strategy for a smooth sale. Most of her business is repeat and referral which is a true testament to her dedication. You can find her at www.yourcommunityrealestate.com. 905 717 6027 ajones@trebnet.com

Sandra Ivkovic, MOSAIC TOUR Consultants Inc.—You dream. We plan. You go! Welcome to your one stop travel center for all your travel needs! 1041 Avenue Rd, Suite 2, Toronto Ontario, M5P 2K6
Telephone: 416-489-0699 http://mosaictour.net/

Silver Sponsors

Shanin Sohrabi IIC Insurance—Their firm does a wide range of financial planning and estate planning for individuals and corporations. Phone Number: 416-640-2620

ABM Accounting Business Management Inc. specializes in self-employed and small corporations, startups and existing businesses in York Region and GTA. ABM offers full-cycle bookkeeping services, from data entry, payroll services, tax remittances (HST, Payroll Deductions, WSIB), financial analysis, to working papers for the tax accountant. For a free assessment of your accounting and bookkeeping needs, call Gabriela at 416-417-5961 or email to gabyd@rogers.com or visit our website at www.accountingabm.com

Carol Buchinski, Independent Stylist—Nygard Style Direct—She provides personalized home shopping and wardrobe consulting for women through style shows, workshops and in home shopping. Nygard is an iconic Canadian company that has recently branched into direct sales. Now fashion, comfort and perfect fit are delivered directly to your door! cbuchinski@rogers.com 289-231-9411 http://carolbuchinski.nygardstyle.com

Lois Irwin—Learn how you can earn extra income on a part time bases with the worlds largest independent suppler of essential services. Or you could possablly save money on Energy, Internet on both Bell and Rogers service , Anovia Merchant Services, Cell Phone, Vivint Security, for you and your business. For more information please call Lois Irwin 416-697-0463 lois.irwin1@hotmail.com

Heather Di Santo, owner of Di Santo Event Management—has a desire to partner with businesses to create fun, active and engaging events in their communities. Working collaboratively with client representatives, Di Santo Event Management brings clients' visions to life by creating the infrastructure for unique and memorable events that are aligned with their strategic and financial goals. Heather is an outgoing introvert, relationship builder, passionate hockey mom, and runner. 647-996-4794 disantoevents@gmail.com

Gatherings Floral Studio, for their donation of flowers and props for all the photos in this book. 559 Steven Ct #4, Newmarket, ON 905-836-0808

Index

Coming Soon… Spring 2019
Everyday Entertaining

Made in the USA
Middletown, DE
31 October 2017